Purging

Z. Violet

BookLeaf Publishing

Presentation by *BookLeaf Publishing*

Web: www.bookleafpub.com

E-mail: info@bookleafpub.com

ISBN: 9789357213837

First edition 2023

To my mother who I owe my life to and my daughter who IS my life and grounding force.

PREFACE

Like most things in my life, I decided to enter this poetry challenge on a whim, an impulse, a moment of compulsiveness.

Unlike most things in my life, I saw this project to the end. I committed time and effort into it, a surprise even to myself.

I poured out my heart on each page; spilled out all the jumbled thoughts and feelings in my head into words and sentences that (hopefully) make sense and are relatable; a purging, then, of thoughts, feelings, emotions, outrage, hurt.

Chapter 1 – The End

It was the beginning of the end.
The walls came crumbling down, caving in,
The sky collapsed in on itself, came crashing
down.
There was devastation, destruction,
A deafening din,
Riot,
Noise,
Dissent.

Death was noisy.

My body wouldn't accept it at first
My heart screamed in protest,
My brain couldn't compute;
That this could happen to me?
Every nerve fibre in my body screamed no;
"We are okay",
"We can make things work",
"It is not the end".

But it was.

You had made sure of it this time,
There was no coming back from this,

I could not survive it,
I would not survive it.

And then my eyes opened.

Saturday 10th November 2018

Life Wants to Live

Life will do anything to survive;
All life, on all levels, has an innate, desperate desire to Be.

A meagre existence is better than no existence.

Self-preservation exists in all life forms, even within the same life form;
Each fibre of your being selfishly wants to survive independently,
Regardless of the rest of the body.

The small cell won't sacrifice itself for the greater good of the whole body;
Even it wants
To exist,
To just be,
To follow His command,
Life answers to
"Be!" and it is.

The fight for life precedes all else.

Life has a thirst to self-preserve,
We cling to existence,

Latch onto it,
Life itself is desperate to exist.

We know within every cell of our body,
Within every fibre of our being,
Within our soul,
That He has told us to be
And when it comes to it, The Self within each living thing will fight to Be.
This innate instinct for self-preservation is YOU hearing, following, accepting His command.

Beyond the Veil

Crushing Sadness. Debilitating Worry. Grief.
A sad, hollow feeling in the pit of my stomach.
Uncontrollable crying. Loud, anguished sobs,
Being pulled out from deep within me.
There must be something so abhorrent about me
That makes me so detestable and unlovable
That my own husband would do this to me.

I came to and the dams broke open.
All these feelings came rushing simultaneously,
Engulfing me like a tsunami.
So this was what it was like on the other side;
This was life beyond the veil.

At first, I felt like a ghost;
There was this life and then the life before.
I had survived it but I was an empty shell,
My body was an imprint of its former self;
Before and after,
Then and now,
Human and ghost.

****

It takes a lifetime to rebuild after a trauma like this.

Even after so many years,
You will still carry the scars of what happened.
They never quite heal,
The slightest of touch
And the wound is raw again,
The blood seeping out from beneath the thin, tired layer of skin
That has formed over the wound.

I like to think that I'm over it
And sometimes it really feels like I am,
But then I will catch sight of a happy couple walking with their child
And it'll hit me out of nowhere;
Unexpected, surprising, uninvited;
A knife straight to the heart,
It momentarily knocks the wind out of me,
Like a punch to the stomach,
The air becomes solid and my starving lungs don't know how to work.
In that infinite moment,
All sense is lost,
North becomes South,
The ground under my feet gives way,
The sky has fallen,
The stars burn my feet as I try to move forward,
There is earth above me, falling, I am being buried.

My daughter's sad and lonely face is the last thing that I see,
"I wish daddy was here" is the last thing that I hear,
As my lacking hand pulls away from hers.
I am not enough for her,
She needs more,
She needs her father,
She needs a mother who isn't emotionally absent,
She needs a mother who doesn't carry a graveyard
Of broken relationships and unfulfilled promises within her.

I can see the loss in her every day.
She knows there is something missing,
She begs me to be what she needs,
And sometimes I try so hard to,
But,
There is so much grief,
There is so much sadness,
There is so much numbness,
There is so much darkness.
I grieve over and over again,
There is mourning and lamenting,
There is relapsing,
There is guilt, so much guilt.

And I am so, so tired.

Dysfunction

These waters are dark and merciless
They will forgive no one;
Not a soul will escape their murky depths.

****

Sometimes, I am on a merry go round and I can't step off.
I am being passed from pillar to post,
Ricocheting off the walls,
Someone else is in the driver's seat.
I am unable to stop or slow down,
I am moving at 100 miles per hour
Without a moment alone to face my demons.

At other times, I am vegetative;
Surrounded in mess and clutter, no energy to clean,
Meals that go uncooked, the contents of a whole shopping trip
That yet again go in the bin as they've been left for too long,
Waiting for me to feel well enough to use them.
At these times, I can lay frozen in a dark room for 48 hours over the weekend,
Not having the willpower to move.

An angry kaleidoscope of conflicting feelings,
implodes within me,
Sometimes, I am being swallowed under the
tidal wave,
At other times, I am floating numbly, hollowly
by,
Like an empty shell on the surface of the water.
When I am with others, I smile all day, laugh
and chat,
Then I come home and, slump into a heap on the
floor.
I am surrounded by people, endless faces and
bodies,
I see the same haunted look in their eyes,
A look I am familiar with as I see it in the mirror
every day;
We are a nation high on antidepressants, feeling
so low,
But there is still a veil between us all. We are all
completely alone.

Sometimes, I run and run and I see no escape,
I end up back where I started.
At other times, I don't even try to move,
Already feeling like the battle is lost.

Sometimes, it all feels too much,
At other times, it's not enough.
I can never decide which feels worse.

Breaking

It turns out it was attachment and fear rooting
me to you, not love.
Your pull wasn't magnetic; it was nothing to do
with attraction;
It was gravitational, like a black hole, sucking
me in -
Unforgiving, pulverising me into a vapour.
It was fear that I couldn't survive without you,
That I needed you,
That I needed a relationship,
That I couldn't be alone.

But being with you turned out to be the loneliest
I have ever been.

Our relationship was a swamp of toxic waste;
Each of us spewing up venom into the barren
wasteland of our marriage.
We were swimming in the poison, drowning,
Our skins burning, melting away, corroding with
the acid,
Choking on it as we tried to keep our heads
above the surface,
Our insides burning, the putrid smell of singed
flesh choking us,

Our mouths, wide open in horrified screams that couldn't escape our lungs.

Again and again, I looked for my haven within you,
I looked for refuge, safety;
I begged you to take me in,
Or at the very least, grant me momentary respite,
A temporary ceasefire,
A chance to catch my breath,
A chance to treat to my throbbing wounds,
But everything was unrelenting;
You were unforgiving.

Our marriage was a battlefield and I was losing.

You can't live in the mouth of a dragon and not expect to get burned.

I walked away so many times before I finally ended things for good;
Even when I ended it, I wasn't sure if I would have the strength to stay away.
I was a shell of a person, an imprint of a real person;
Going through the motions of life in a dark, despairing stupor.
I knew I didn't want to return to you. Why was it so hard then?

Why did walking away feel like I was wading through treacle?

Awakening

One day I woke up and I wasn't sad anymore.
I wish it was as easy as that;
So many times I wished it would happen this way;
That the horrible weight in the pit of my stomach,
The constricting of my tired heart,
The cloud of fog constantly shrouding my thoughts
And the bile constantly leaving a bitter taste in my throat,
Would dissipate and squander away like the unwelcome guests that they were.

Slowly, the fog started to lift.
There was still a numbness and gloom,
I still had complete breakdowns sometimes,
But I kept myself busy with life;
Gradually starting to feel slightly okay.

So, here is my
Mostly-Dysfunctional-and-Partly-Acceptable recipe for feeling kind of okay:

- Therapy – As many sessions as I was allowed. It didn't 'fix me' as I had hoped, but it helped
- Binge Eating – until my weight ballooned, but food was my sanctuary
- Saying 'Yes' to More Things – every opportunity and new experience
- Trying a New Hobby - painting, writing occasionally, nothing that required commitment
- Getting back to work after a very long career break, building a life for myself and becoming financially independent
- Getting a house and making a home and a family
- Obsessively reading about how to be a better parent and trying to implement

Working on my spirituality

- Doing bare minimum, letting everything go
- A whole load of procrastination and allowing myself to be excused
- Taking every opportunity to overcome my social anxiety
- Talking to my child; trying valiantly to be her source of emotional anchorage and healthy conversation, even though I felt dead inside

- Hugging my child every day, even when I didn't want to
- Building a wall a mile high around me to keep myself safe
- Keeping everyone at arm's length to avoid being stung
- Lighting all the candles
- Buying all the fairy lights
- Binge watching every series I liked each night
- Indulging in every treat that I could think of

The first few years after The End,
I kept myself busy with these things
And slowly, the frost began to thaw,
There was still numbness and darkness,
Sometimes, I would feel a prickling behind my eyes,
Or lump in my throat,
But the cogs began to slowly shift,
The Awakening had begun;
The clouds had slowly started to move,
And a watery sun had begun to shine down.

Demons

My demons and I are old acquaintances,
I have known them all my life,
They have been with me from childhood.

They have watched me grow, and become who I am,
They have celebrated my every failure
And commiserated every success.

Sometimes they watch from the side-lines, sneering and mocking,
At other times, they laugh in my face, blatantly rebuking.
I see them whispering about me behind their hands with contempt,
All my endeavours are tainted with their doubt and derision.

Often times, they have stolen my sleep,
Loudly reproaching me again and again, robbing me of rest.

Their commitment to me has been so strong,
They have been with me when even my closest have left me.

Their presence has been unwavering,
Their influence has painted my life with their hues,

And sometimes, I fear that I will be buried with them.

DNA

I sing the song of my mothers before me,
They composed elaborate laments of loss,
wanting, sacrifice, betrayal.

Though they have long since passed,
Their haunting notes have travelled through
eternities,
Passed through generations,
Defied time and space,
Resonating despite the hands around their
throats that wanted to silence them.

They manifest in the vibrations of my each and
every cell.
When I become still and listen,
I can hear the hum of every cell echoing their
lament.

Building from the Ground Up

I am building my fortress around me;
I am the architect, the designer and the builder.

I start with the foundations – I build those from
all the lessons learned from people's lies and
unfulfilled promises, 'trust no one', it says on
every slab of concrete.

The support beams are made from the steal of
my resolve and the warrior spirit of my heart
that has turned to hard stone – 'I will not let you
destroy me again'.

I make each brick myself; I mix the clay of sheer
effort with the grit of determination and let them
bake for 5 days in the heat of my anger, scorn
and heartbreak.

I construct the walls, laying one brick at a time,
one on top of the other. Each brick carries a
different commandment, a different rule – 'thou
shalt, thou shalt not; I must, I must not'.

The mortar that glues the bricks together is made
of my overwhelming fear that another

catastrophe like this cannot happen again – 'I cannot survive something like this again'.

The last thing I build is the roof. I weave a tapestry of all my failures, all my regrets, all my disappointments. I spread it overhead and bury myself beneath it.

Finally, I retreat to deep within the bowels of my fortress.
I take myself to the darkest corner of the darkest room and take root there.
It is uninviting, it is cold, it is gloomy.
Even in the middle of summer, it feels barren and icy.

This is where I stay.

Building from the Sky Down

How can you build when you're buried beneath the ground?
How can you build when you're crumbling before you've even began?
How can you reconstruct when you've been floored?
All your designs and constructions will be tainted with dejection.

I tried valiantly to get up, to climb, to elevate.
I tried physically; I looked after my health and tried to keep moving.
I tried mentally; I got a job, I got therapy.
I tried spiritually; I would talk about keeping the faith whilst being at peace with one's destiny.

I tried to let go of all the hurt and anger that I held within me.
I tried valiantly to be kinder to myself, to show myself compassion,
I tried to forgive those who had hurt me.
I tried to purge out all the venom,
I tried to let it all go
And cleanse myself from within.

I scrubbed the curse words that had been scrawled onto the walls of my fortress,
I repainted the walls in bright, vibrant colours instead of the grey that I had grown accustomed to.
I laid down soft carpets where the hard, splintered floorboards had been.
I ventured out from the dungeons and explored the chambers above,
I opened the windows and invited the sunshine to stream in,
I let the soft breeze float in through the open doors and breathed the vitality into my cold bones.

This time, my goal was to reach the top, reach the sky and to build from the sky downwards.
I tried to undo the lifetime of toxic thinking and emotional malnourishment.
I had made little progress; there was still a long way to go, but I closed my eyes, opened my arms and let hope and faith carry me out on the wings of a butterfly and take me towards the sun.

I landed on a cloud and begun to build my castle in the sky.

Yo-Yo

I progress, I relapse, I progress I relapse,
I go up, I go down,
I have peaks, I have troughs,
One step forward, two steps back,
I have become so familiar with this dance.

It's like I am a Yo-yo, my demons are in control,
I'm a prisoner to them, they are the guards on patrol.
I am dangling from a string that is wound tightly around;
I try to move forwards but I am yanked back – to them I am bound,
Sometimes I manage to get a fair distance away,
I think I've escaped, I'm free, it's a new day,
Just as I'm about to slow down my pace,
I am kicked back into my place,
I belong to my fears, they rule this land,
And every time, I walk back into the palm of their waiting hand.

A Fairy Tale

It was a fairy tale - this was my chapter,
The one where the girl finds her prince and lives happily ever after.

****

My knight in shining armour came,
One day on horseback, whispering my name.

I loved the way you said it, like it was a sacred word,
"At last", I thought, "it was my turn".

I met you on my birthday, the year I turned 23,
The best birthday gift, in your hand you held the key.

You unlocked the chains around my heart, you could unravel every knot,
You broke the door to the chamber holding me prisoner, removed every block.

You said all the right things and gave all the right answers,
I lapped it all up, I was powerless against your advances.

I drank in all your words, believed every lie,
I couldn't say no, didn't even want to try.

"I have been searching for you all my life", you
said,
I closed my eyes, exhaled slowly; from now on,
only you existed in my head.

Sweet temperament, sweet words, sweet
innocence – that's what I could see,
I was not used to mild men, but you were like
honey.

I closed my mouth and let my heart speak;
This is what euphoria felt like, and I was at the
peak.

It felt like I was flying, my soul was so high,
I was soaring, freely amongst the stars in the
night sky.

My heart danced, beat against my ribs, waltzing
to your tune,
I was your puppet, I was your subject, but I felt
like your muse.

I was besotted; drawn to you like a moth to the
flame,

And I would willingly burn myself, unaware of your game.
I wondered how I had been so lucky, to land the lead role in this fairy tale,
You were my healing balm, the cure to each and every ail.

I would have gone to the ends of the earth for you,
Followed you into oblivion, destroyed myself for you.

I built all my foundations on the thorny bed of your lies,
Unaware of the prickling as I went down to lie.

I was blind to the shackles as they slowly crept up,
And bound my arms and legs until it was too late, time was up.

It was round one, I was stuck in your game,

That's when I realised;
Sometimes
The prince
And the villain
Are one
And the same.

Flashbacks

I am 3 and my earliest memory is of me
screaming
As my father drops me off to nursery,
The teacher prying my fingers apart from my
father's as I thrash and plead.

I am 4 and I spend my playtimes sitting alone on
the steps of the playground,
Whilst all the children play around me.
I watch as they laugh and run, feeling so
removed from them.

I am 5 and all I see is my mother crying
And my father perpetually angry.
You can see the sadness in the eyes of my
siblings,
And the wildness they've developed from living
in a lion's den,
And having to be heard in a family of 11.

I am 6 and I am so afraid of the dark,
I cling on to my father's body at night to keep
away the demons
That are lurking just out of sight.

I am 7 and I can't understand why I keep being scolded and humiliated by everyone.
I live in perpetual fear of being reprimanded.

I am 9 and I spend all night awake,
Only falling asleep when the sun comes up.
I have developed an extreme fear of the dark and of the night
And I have lost my ability to sleep.

I am 13 and I chase the high of mischief, being free and finally being accepted.
I have friends that fulfil my urge for causing riot and being seen.
I live for the adrenaline rush that comes with being a rebellious teenager.

I am 16 and on the brink of so much potential;
My high school years have been exhilarating, empowering.
I am braced to go out and seize the day. The world is my oyster.

I am 17, at college, no friends, an outsider again.
I don't belong, I don't fit in and I'm always tired.
I do badly in my exams, all my ambitions and plans fall through.

I am 18. I arrive at my last-choice university
doing my last-choice degree.
I am a fish out of water; I don't fit in and I don't
want to be there.

I am 20 and I am still a child.
I try valiantly to conform, become part of
society.
But I don't belong anywhere.

I am 23. I meet a man and I fall in love.
I feel content and fulfilled for the first time in
my whole life.
For the first time ever, life feels good.

I'm 25 and everything is in tatters;
Failed career, failed marriage, failed life.
There has been a war and I have barely survived.

I am 30 and I'm standing amongst the rubble
and ruins of a lifetime of dysfunction.
I look around, surveying the damage and wonder
how I will ever get on my feet.

I look down at two, wide, innocent eyes staring
at me, reflecting the doom that I see around.
Those eyes are imploring me, pleading with me
to pick things up and restore order.

But all I know is chaos and entropy
And all I attract is disorder.

Fronts and Fault Lines

I have perfected my mask,
I have chiselled away at it, carved it
spectacularly,
It has been thirty years in the making.
I have created an elaborate and layered work of
art,
Used only the finest materials and the most
specialised tools.

It is a thing to be marvelled at.
It has fooled every visitor at every gallery;
It is a regular feature in exhibits, and
There is not a single person who has had the eye
to see
Or the intuition to become aware of
The fault lines that are entrenched deep into the
planes of the mask,
The craters that have formed when the meteor
hit,
The superficiality of the too-enthusiastic smile,
carved forcefully into the mask,
The hollows behind the eye sockets,
The brittleness of the plaster, stretched thin and
dry.

Fantasies

I walk in to a home full of lightness and laughter,
It is my home,
I have a proper family,
There is warmth,
There is healthy conversation,
I hear the murmur of light, happy chatter.
No one is shouting,
I'm not crying.
My child has siblings; she isn't lonely,
I can hear my children laughing,
My husband is present and supportive,
I am secure in his presence,
The past few years never happened;
He never cheated on me,
He never lied to me,
He never controlled me,

He never hit me.

All the things he told me about loving me were true.
My child is free of the trauma of coming from a broken home,

She is free of the trauma of having a mum who isn't emotionally present,
She doesn't tell me she misses dad,
She doesn't tell me she wants dad to come,
She doesn't ask me why her daddy doesn't live with her like everyone else's,
Her dad is here to tuck her into bed,
He is here to put her to sleep, stroking her hair and holding her tight.
She does not carry the pain of previous generations,
When I look into her eyes, I do not see my own hollowness looking back at me.
My mother is here, present, happy, light.
She is free of her shackles,
I am free of mine.
She has lived a life she deserves;
She has been adored and appreciated by my father,
I have learnt how to love properly from both of them.
She isn't an empty shell of a woman,
Whose only aim is to serve and bow down.
My children are happy,
I am enough for them,
I am enough for my husband,

And my heart is full.

Me

I don’t know who I am.

When I look in the mirror,
I see a stranger looking back at me.
I don’t love her;
I don’t really know what I feel for her,
Except sometimes pity
And mostly self-loathing.

Why did you say that?
Why did you do this?
You always do that;

You’re a loser.

My therapist asks me:
“If you saw your younger self walk in through the door,
What would you say to her?”
I pause at that.
I’ve had 30 years of life experience,
30 years which feels like centuries of bad choices and catastrophes,
But I still don’t have any advice for my younger self

I haven't learnt anything from the mistakes,
I haven't evolved,
I've just slowly frozen over,
Like something left out, forgotten about in a blizzard.
I am numb a lot of the time and unstable when I'm not,
Emotional dysregulation, they call it.
Maybe that's why I'm still stuck in the rut of a bad marriage 4 years later,
Unable to separate myself from him for fear of what will happen if I do.
Maybe that's why I still get myself in situations
Where I have no control and no say in the outcome.

My therapist says that healing can't happen until you show yourself compassion;
Until you start believing that you deserve better
And that you don't deserve the things that happened to you,

But it all sounds so strange and foreign.

Mother

She is home,
She is a safe place,
She is the root that keeps you grounded,
She is the anchor that holds you steady in the midst of a storm.

She is familiar,
She is safe,
She is the land to which you can always return.

She is love, she is light,
She is fierce, she is dark,
She is the dawn that breaks after a dark night,
She is the birdsong on a summer's morning.

She is my moon and my stars,
She is the sun that warms me from inside,
She is the strength I carry within me,
That keeps me going long after I would have given up.

She is sacrifice and pain,
She carries deep hurt within her,
Life has not been good to her,
People have not been good to her,

All she has known is sacrifice, pain,
Enduring without complaint.
She is innocence and simplicity,
She is a queen, beneath whose feet lies my heaven.

For all the things she didn't receive in this world and all the sacrifices she made,
May she receive tenfold in paradise.
May the angels of heaven say her name and welcome her,
May there be a special place for her amongst all the special women of paradise;
Women who went hungry so that the stomachs of their children could be full,
Women who endured abuse and mistreatment so that their children could have a roof over their heads and a bed to sleep in.
Women who sacrificed their today's for the tomorrow's of their children,

I am swimming in a sea of opportunity and abundance. All I have is due to you and your prayers.
Thank you.

Father

Sacrifice, sheer effort, living on the bare minimum,
Travelling 4000 miles to the other side of the world to give his children a better life.

Loneliness, racism, the children of white people vandalising his already-broken rented room,
Shouting insults at him as they walked past.

Cold, so cold, bone-penetratingly deep. The winters were so cold and his lodgings were bare; dripping roof, no heating, cold damp walls and draughty windows.

Staying hungry, surviving on one meal a day, sending every meagre penny he made back home to feed the ever-hungry mouths of his waiting children and to pay for the medicines of his ill parents.

Enduring, enduring, and enduring. Accepting everything, suffering silently, not breathing a word to anyone, not even in the eye of the storm.

****

It's very hard to write about you;
It's very hard to know how to put into words
such a complex, conflicting person,
Immortalise your intricacies and contradictions
onto a page and
Condense a lifetime of being you into a few
words.

My earliest feelings towards you were of fear,
love, respect, confusion.
My earliest memories of you are of looking up at
this tall, towering man,
(Who actually isn't very tall at all),
And being so sure that you were a man of
immense strength and power.
But I also remember your hugs and your
softness.
I remember you giving me the physical love that
I so craved as a child;
When my mother was emotionally absent and
couldn't show affection,
You at least showed me the closest thing to what
a child thinks is love.
Your hugs were life-giving, nourishing,
replenishing, my life-force.
I felt so safe and happy in your arms. I felt so
special.
You would put me to sleep at night,

Holding me tight to keep the fear at bay.
You filled my need for hugs and kisses,
And showered me with your love and attention.

But I was scared of you as well.
You were not a man to be crossed,
You were short-tempered, quick to anger,
You had very strict expectations
And I knew not to cross the line.
At the same time, you would cry at a TV programme.
I often wondered how someone so strong and fearful,
Who could handle anything, could become emotional like that.

Being vulnerable and weak was a luxury you couldn't afford.
You were too busy bearing the weight of responsibility
And fulfilling the needs of so many
To show a moments weakness or stop to catch your breath.

As I grew older,
You seemed to grow shorter.
I saw you make mistakes and realised you're human, just like me.

I saw your vulnerabilities and realised you hurt,
just like anyone else.

You spent a lifetime building for your children,
You finally managed to bring them to you,

So why does it feel like are still 4000 miles
away?

Motherhood

It was love at first sight.

Small, round face, chubby, flushed cheeks,
The smallest, tiniest thing,
Little hands curled into a fist,
Tiny fingers holding mine.

Holding you tight to my chest as you nuzzled in,
Your skin was so soft, delicate, fragile - like touching rose petals,
Your gossamer strands of silky hair lay on your small round head,
Your eyes were squeezed tightly shut,
Your long wispy lashes framing them.

Your chin was the cutest thing, pointy and soft,
I would tip your head back to kiss it.
Your neck was so small and fragile;
I would nestle into it on long, dark nights,
Inhaling that sweet milky smell that only newborns have.

You fit on my forearm,
Tiny body curled into a ball,

I would rub your back with just two fingers to burp you;
Milk-drunk face in my hands,
Squashy cheeks between my fingers.

The first time you opened your wide eyes, you looked up at me, studying me intently. Mummy. I was your mummy.

****

It wasn't normal tiredness.
It was crushing, all-consuming, exhausting tiredness,
Waves of sleepiness washing over me,
Again and again,
Burying me deeper and deeper.

Wading through treacle.

Every movement felt like wading through treacle,
So strenuous, draining the life out of me,
My body was leaden,
The weight of responsibility,
Of sleep-deprivation,
Of complete, sheer exhaustion,
Weighing down on my shoulders,
Forcing me down,

Deeper and deeper into the depths of the ocean.

My insides felt so raw.
Everything closing in from above, beneath, all sides, crushing me.
The first few months felt like an endless cycle
Of feeding, being sick, nappy change, soiled clothes,
Feeding, being sick, nappy change, soiled clothes,
Feeding, being sick, nappy change, soiled clothes.

All night long.

All night long.

All. Night. Long.

Until the sun came up.

The newborn nappies were too large for your body,
Your clothes would get soiled each time you relieved yourself.
The prospect of having to face going out with you,
To the shop next door felt like climbing Everest.

The washing machine was broken,
 so as soon as it hit morning,
I would wash all the soiled babygrows and vests by hand,
Drying them frantically over a heater
In time for it all to begin again as the night closed in.

On the 5th night, I began to hallucinate.
On the 6th night, I became hysterical,
Convinced that I had forgotten how to sleep,
When I was finally offered a rare moment of respite,
I found that I couldn't even close my eyes;
Sheer panic glued them awake
And the guilt rose up from within me like a tsunami.
I had developed extreme paranoia, literally overnight, that SIDS would take you.

You had severe reflux and colic,
You couldn't lay on your back for any length of time,
I would spend the entire night holding you,
Fighting off sleep,
Simultaneously feeling like I was going to slip into a coma from the exhaustion,
Terrified that if I blinked for too long, I would be unable to open my eyes again.

Some nights you would feed for the entire night long.
Cluster feeding, they called it. Growth spurts.
How many growth spurts can one baby have, I'd think.
Those first few months felt like one continuous growth spurt,
Night after night of cluster feeding until morning,
When you'd finally seem full for an hour or so,
Before crying and rooting for milk again.

I feel honoured to have had the experience of being your mum,
But I will never forget the hardship and the price
I had to pay to be able to earn that title.

Acceptance

I tell myself to just accept things.
I must withstand, I must keep going,
I must stop fighting, objecting, protesting;

Life cannot endure through resistance.

I tell myself to just accept that which I cannot
control;
Only then can I be at peace.
I tell myself to be surrender to what has
happened.
I tell myself to make peace with my past,
I tell myself to be ready for and at peace with
situations outside my control that are still to
come.
I try to accept my circumstances, accept my
situation, accept myself.

There is sweetness in surrender.

I tell myself to become still;
To stop resisting and fighting against the current;
To float on the surface of the water of life and let
it take me where it will.

I try to become like the water; moving with the current, not against it,
Flowing over the pebbles in my path, going around any obstacles that threaten to stop me.
I try to convince myself that accepting life's tests and trials is not weakness; it is strength.

I must nurture and celebrate the force within me that endures past all of life's challenges.

I become still like a statue and try to practice the art of just doing nothing.
I will my heart to stop feeling; my brain to stop thinking.
I tell myself that not everything needs a reaction,
Not every life event needs a response.
I am not what has happened to me,
And anyway, things don't happen to us, they happen for us.
Every storm we weather is designed to smooth out the roughness.
I tell myself to welcome the waves that crash against me with open arms,
I tell myself to ride the tide.
How long can I fight against things?
How long can I try to control what is outside my control?

Most of all, I tell myself to accept the stranger in
the mirror;
I have treated her like a pariah all life long.
I have blamed her, scalded her, abused her.
I have not been kind to her.
Her deepest wounds are self-inflicted.
I tell myself to accept her,
Warts and all.
With every fault, every scar and every part of
ugly that resides within her.
I look at her in the mirror.

"I'm sorry", I say.

A prayer

I pray for peace,
I pray for safety,
I pray for contentment.

I pray for my daughter to always be under Your protection,
I pray that she remains upon Your guidance through her life.
I pray that she grows up to be a good person,
A kind human, a compassionate friend, an empath who helps the world to heal.

I pray for strength and resolve.
I pray for surrender and acceptance of what is to come.
I pray for an integrity that always pushes me to choose the right path,
Even when I may be tempted otherwise.

I pray for softness and a generous heart,
I pray for a sincerity that allows me to forgive freely,
To love fearlessly, to hope again and again.

I pray for my mother and father,
I pray for their health, I pray for their happiness.
I pray for them to attain heaven.
I pray for family and all my loved ones.
I pray for us all to be under His shelter and
mercy.

I pray for the world;
It is in a state of turmoil.
I pray for humanity;
There is so much loss and sadness.
There is so much evil that we have committed
with our own hands.

I am homesick for the place where my soul is
from,
I pray to be worthy of returning there again.

I pray to be the kind of person who is worthy of
Your heaven,
And I pray to be there with all my loved ones
one day.

www.ingramcontent.com/pod-product-compliance
Lightning Source LLC
Chambersburg PA
CBHW051737130826
49812CB00033B/903
* 9 7 8 9 3 5 7 2 1 3 8 3 7 *